ONLY THE BRAVE

Shahanaz M Meera

ISBN 978-93-5610-683-3

Published in India 2022 by Pencil

A brand of
One Point Six Technologies Pvt. Ltd.
123, Building J2, Shram Seva Premises,
Wadala Truck Terminal, Wadala (E)
Mumbai 400037, Maharashtra, INDIA
E connect@thepencilapp.com
W www.thepencilapp.com

Author biography

Shahanaz M Meera grew up in the Southern side of India, Growing up, she was captivated with Cricket, this interest led to some early exposure to reading since she was drawn to stories related to Cricket. A certain interest in poetry arose by the time around 2017 when she used to scribble random poems out of nowhere and this led to a constructive phase in her poetry. A Software Engineer at the moment, writing poems turned out to be a passion upon which she is trying to succeed. Recently, her first-ever poetry collection named TORN got published which is indeed the beginning of a milestone ahead.

CONTENTS

Epigraph

"Love him and let him love you. Do you think anything else under heaven really matters?" – James Baldwin

Preface

" You told me of the stars and the rainbow, I'm here somewhere afar from the ground searching for you in the crowds, I cannot find, these lights blinded my vision, these heights took off the ladder, how will I come down, will there ever be a chance?. Please search for me and find me, this life it's not all it's cracked up to be "

Acknowledgements

I decided to try and write a book about two individuals who directly or indirectly changed many people's lives time after I got to know them better. There were already a considerable number of books written for them, but yet a poetry collection was never there. I asked myself this question a couple of times and always ended up giving a, yes, probably this needs to be done. I have learned about their life a little more than I already knew, read, and watched. It painted me a picture that wasn't already there. I have had suggestions on how to improve the book, and how to make it sound like a story, a life, and give it life. Most of them, I've written with a paper and a pen, in a calm and quiet place so that I could really indulge in what I really wanted. It took me a lot of time to develop the storyline, it started off with drawing some random pictures and arranging them, so they would make sense. I'm very grateful to my sister Shermina M Meera for the constant support she has been giving me from the very beginning. I'm very thankful to all those lovely people who read my previous work and all those who gave feedback on it. I can guarantee you that, this is deeper and once you start reading, you will feel it in your chest.

Shahanaz M Meera

If Loneliness Had a NAME

The September nights have been starryblazed in the raven darknessholding the veil above like a picture-perfect memory from the past,transparent the sky has been, showing me the countsI'll never be able to count down.

The breeze walked past me, telling me to followwhat is left behind, the gale I had in mewhispered " it's time, it's been long"
I looked out the windowlike the sun peeking out of the clouds

I cannot pretend to have not seen "us"invisible aside, still visible to all.inaudible to only us, still audible to all.We walked away, hands apart, eyes on the horizon,
promising without a promise.It's safe, not to revisitwe both guaranteed to mute,it went from a safe place to the scariest.

If loneliness had a name, I'd have called itby what this is, you always say it is what it is.I pick the phone at timesremembering not to dial it again,We were wrong in this battlenone of us were qualified enough to say" I won ", we waited for the "We" or "Us"which was crossed by the inkof " let's give it a time", and the clock is deadIt's still paused on the moment we left

I'm searching for the sunto follow the shadow, to tell mewhere the hour hand should be.
When in darkness, I followed the noonthat just faded away, it's reaching tomorrow,
I know you won't forget.It's the loneliest twenty-eighthI've ever been to, I cannot hear youscreaming from the next door,or at least through the phone call.

" It would've been easier to ignore if it was not you and not me. This number wouldn't be on our charts if this wasn't for us. I miss the colors in you, how you simplified the affection with just a smile, hiding behind your words. I'm staring into this display, dreaming of answering the call, I'm not making it so is you. Are we tired!! Should we let go? "

In the SAME PAGE

He is getting thinner these daysthere is a wound, spreading through every nervethat I cannot heal.Sleep, he is not finding it,
avoiding it in all possible ways.

He is not hungry, eyes are wet every day,
still not pouring.The rush of blood hasn't steadied,
it's still on the high tide.If there is something he needs to utter,
that too never came out.

Converging the days into this phase,
counting down the daysas if there is no change,I'm hoping
he would be openso I can place my arms on his chest
and tell him to be strong

" Listen to me boo, you need to stay strong "

He was the star to my skythe depth of my ocean,
the hilltop of my expectations.
I was knitting this story once,
the thread is broken now,

I'm trying to tie it together,
but I can't. I'm not strong enough like he said,
there is not enough space to let you into this.

I'll survive this alone, leave a note on the door,
I'll read it when it's long gone.
Fire, it's burning in my chest,
there is only one thought, and I cannot think it through.
Maybe I'll survive, maybe not.
I won't ask for a hand to hold,
let's give it a time as I said.

The sky is cloudy, it's darkening day by day.
I haven't seen the sunrise,
the sun hasn't come up these days,
for me, it's all rainy and I don't see a seasonal change.
Hunger doesn't bother me anymore,
neither the sleep nor the waking-ups.
when the final note is here, maybe I won't sing...
I hope you understand, maybe not.

" I'm not strong enough love, I don't think I'll ever be "

Birthday Cake

I wanted to wish, but I didn't,In your eyes, I've seen the world evading,
pages furling, love retreating, a smile pretending.In your voice, I've heard the cry of a tiny bird,
looking for its mother to come home and feed him,like she used to when he was young.

This day peeps in, in this nest,
you have people underneath your chest to look after,
some cries to shush, some stomach to feed.
Armed around the problemsyou face it like a friend, conversing like in a casual talk.

This felt nothing special
there were no cakes, no balloons
I remember it's not like the last winter
some faces left behind,
it disappeared, I found no words to
sing you the birthday song
I couldn't see you standing still.

You stood close to the telephone,
it rang already thrice this morning,
not the voice you wished to hear,
there is no way I can tell you to bear

this loneliness in your chest.
The day that she left, you just didn't knowthat she was going somewhere you couldn't go.

It followed the pattern,
you smiling over the cloudy curtains,
staging yourself in a solo act
where you laugh aloud as if
its life and we should face it as such,
but deep inside, there is a crash of waves
against the solid rocks
hurting yourself in ways no one knows of.

The tide goes out, it comes inthe rain pours down, you didn't drench,you were soaked in pain all over againbut still shone like the morning sun rays.

I've seen you drowning in this oceanyet again you swam across the depthand made it steady, made it easier.

You found strength amidst this weaknessa heal to the wound,but there is nothing that will curethe pain you are going to bear from now on.I wish I could tell youthis shall too pass, but I didn'tI only looked into your eyes,and you were already talking in emotionsin letterless words, in wordless sentences

" I knew the length of this missing, he buried his vision to the green floor mat on the kitchen, wiping one or two tears off his cheeks as he looked away from my side. He needed that space, that time alone, I choose to stay out of there for a few minutes, so he could pick the pieces together again "

Should I go out and smile likeI used to, and pretend that it's easy?I have walked past that path alreadywandered in emptiness, with a half-empty heartand a full broken mind, the glass piecespierced into my throat, I no longer wish to talk.Silence, it begins with me and ends with me,maybe this is all I wish for,some, time alone, to visit some closed doorsto let alone sleep in its armsto talk to only that image unseen.

I cried over a broken teacup today,
having it seated between the sink and my right arm
where I was lost in the depth
of a nightmare, it slipped from my hand
reached the floor with a thud.
Life, I've seen it flashing before my eyes,
for the face I'm searching
It is immersed in the invisibility,
I wish I could be invisible too.

Lost in the middle of an unrewarded chase
where she was my anchor and compass,
This Saturday morning, 9:15 AM
I longed for a phone call, and to hear her voice
but it rang, the voice wasn't the same.
I picked the phone, this time dialed the number,
I stopped after the first ring, what if she don't pick up
at least I can pretend, she didn't because I hung up.

" I lost my mom, a lost sock can be found,
but this void, it cannot be filled "

A challenge to put my shoes on again,to keep the house in order,to send the high waves to a full restto laugh aloud, even when it's burning inside.
I saw you gazing into my side,
there is no birthday cake, like the last time

I felt myself curling up intothis loneliness, with doors, shut ahead of me,with conversations, inaudibleI fake this existence, I feel long gone.
These tears maybe cheap,
even days of sorrow is a heap.
I still stand, closer to the sinkwhere I expect my memories to ink" Where do broken hearts go?"

" I didn't look back, I shut the door and immersed myself in the kitchen, where I and my mom spend most of the moments together. The dull grey walls shifted, my eyes chose the nothingness. Some time alone was all I needed, he knew it without even telling. An hour or two, passed, still I didn't count, no one knocked, or I pretended they didn't. "

.

Christmas Eve

It is not just Christmas eve,
but his birthday too.
As the forenoon went all gloomy
like the petals in a funeral
I arranged the tabletop
with roses and candles
spreading the fragrance of peace
and love all across the room.

As he opened the Kitchen door,
after almost two hours
his eyes were still not in the picture.
When the sun goes down in your life
you feel positively empty,
everything stops and is misplaced.
A hard realization dawns,
that you are now alone.

Every tear you dropped the other days
may return as uninvited guests,
shush my love, I'm here to wipe it away.
I kept decorating the table,
I didn't want the gloominess
to cloud again in his face.

The clouds bathed in sunrays
trees reaching the sky ahead,
the lunchtime easily disappeared.
leaving both of us alone in the dining room.
It was awaiting us to behold,
to point to the stars which are
ready to appear within a few hours' time.

"What do you prefer! A walk? "
A questionnaire slipped out without my concern,
it didn't extend to another,
Was it audible? I was unsure.
He was searching for a pattern
on the floor, the chequered one.
"Yeah Yeah", answer and a nod
It was audible enough for me.

We didn't extend our arms
it was already connected somehow,
where my pinky finger would search for his
it would curl up along.
The outpoured affection,
composed within ' We are alright '
finally surrendered.
Having chosen this moment,
memories blew back at me
the ' KIss me you fool '
always been the beginning of something.

Faught, taught, and caught
between our arms, our hearts
wandered like a refugee,

where every conversation we revisited
had a story to tell us too.
" I was hoping... one day "
It didn't complete, I knew I shouldn't

" Every incomplete sentence in our conversation knew, we were keeping those for other days around. Sometimes, all the words left unsaid will form as a wound, unhealed. I never thought the words we kept within ourselves even though we wanted to let out, at the end of the day will eventually break the peace, I'm afraid to stay silent, maybe that silence will be the most hurting emotion of an individual "

The tall grass, skyward gaze
face to face words exchanging,
with his back touching the ground
breeze caressing his hair, the ticklish feather
We've seen the future of this
somewhere afar, without telling, only knowing.

As we set our eyes on the horizon
it went back to its home
leaving both of us there drenched in crimson red
The Christmas lights were seen
on the town a few miles away
The stars portrayed a picture
seen by millions, known only by a few
Truth, we never let it out
even though it was already visible in our eyes

" We stood, craving for an untouched beginning, to warm each other in our hugs like we used to, to fly wherever we want to, to be seen by none, to have our own moment, not captured by anyone, to set the 'no's on fire, to set ourselves free, I don't know where to begin, how to begin, everything feels pointless"

Our eyes together met the stars
time flew by like a Peregrine Falcon
diving into our silence filled conversation.
" Happy birthday and Merry Christmas Boo "
as I opened the blue-paper wrapped
box, adorned in ribbon and bows
I left a sigh of relief
I've seen the smile
slipping out from the corners
of his lips, after a long run.

" The calmness of a twenty-five-year-old, the cheeky grin of a six-year-old - it flashed in his eyes. As he opened the present with the same old look I've seen all these years, I never thought he would be sodden in the rain of tears, blurring his vision. He buried his face into my chest, my heart was pounding in his ears. I wrapped my arms around him, promising to not let go, without a word, without a promise. It felt as if the world was slowing down, it went to a pause. A silver key with blue and green design on it, a new home, to cease his sadness, to regain at least the happiness... "

New Year Never Came

Another year, waited on the doorstep
I didn't utter the word welcome
The one in the room
was ready to leave,
Neither did I say goodbye
nor did I invite the one on the steps
it swung the door open,
walked past me without looking.

I didn't consider this would pass
A year ahead,
like a wet summer,
like an unwanted horn
Didn't ask why it arrived so fast.
Like an unspoken guest, it looked at me
I saw a life sighing without direction
None realized whether it was mine or his

I did not want to flood him with grief again
Let the thunderstorm come and go
My breath won't let him
to soak into it.
I've seen a crying little boy in him

chased by the thief whose eyes were full all day.
Even the arrows aimed elsewhere hit us
and it was like a thunderbolt,
we promised not to surrender.

Let time change,
let the flowers bloom,
I'll bring the days back to him
It's been six years since we were trapped
in a vast net
smothered by the deeds.
To hide between the pages,
to turn and to smile
we've got memories
No tears shed, or
maybe no one has seen it
cause you wiped it away.

Will the guest in front
immersed in the paint of another year
write new pages of survival?
A burden of questions,
unanswered in the corner.
Even if my torrent would turn into a flood
I'll keep him aside,
untouched and safe from
the distance afar.

With Love

For all the dried up TEARS

The words connected
having it written with the blank ink
it continued to tell me a story,
I scribbled, it wasn't uniform
it didn't form a picture
but I could feel myself in there.
The extended curls were gone,
I kept my thoughts sink in his eyelashes
all the dried up tears left a stain on his face
when you look, you'll see the blankness
I sensed it too,
I painted it in my words too.

Talks, the late counts never had it enough
we were full of ears, but sentences were shut in voice.
It's been almost three months
I've seen his face getting dull, day by day.
He used to throw the smile away
as if it was an intruder.
He never refused to pretend that
he was alright, at least when I was in the scene.

" It was the sign of the times, and we knew. He wiped those tears away this time, setting everything right "

I bought him a black long coat
having seen his hair cut down
I knew he'd miss it
It's only a few months,
but I miss him already.
The gravity pulled me to the ground
from a ten top tower
when he was pulled up,
wings stretched, a revert in gravitation.
He walked, the grasses outgrew
so does my thought.

We should be having the sign of the times
but the sign got broke
where the up turned down, and the opposite.
For me and mom, your's was the song
it wasn't engraved on the walls
but in my heart.
Circulated till I hit the floor
arms across my chest, within your hold.
You held me closer to heal the wound,
and all I did was build the walls higher

" I build my walls higher, letting everyone out of my sight. At least for once, I counted you in that chart "

To Begin AGAIN

For a while, the doors were closed
eyes were shut behind the darkness
words were drowning in the pointlessness
there was this space between your inhale and exhale
which I used to cover without a fear
amidst the fall and spring
we lived and died in silence
there was no rendezvous in the hallways.

Today is the twelfth of May
a remembrance of how we wandered
like the ghosts invisible to one another
how we looked without looking
talked without talking
everything is painted in the sky
where they've captured only the two of us.

How to say, you are my sweetest creature
like William Shakespeare once said
Cry 'O sweet creature!' and then kiss me hard
Oh the Daffodils to my heart
let's begin again
from a land which was left as such
from the lost words searching for a tag
from a mirror that reflects only us

from the chambers which were forbidden to us.

" You know I write too many songs about you "

Those tunes returned me to the rhythm
which was out of sync for a long time.
I recalled the dining table conversations we used to have
from my first ever meal to this
and how it still remains my favorite of all.
When you sang my lyrics
and named it a fruit, I was a Dad,
they made me consider myself one.

We will walk down the garden hand in hand
on the aisle, we will wear each other's names
the lifetime bond is unbreakable they say
I agree without having another word in it.
Where one line is quoted on yours
and I quote it with only this "
these imprintings on skin
are for the life ahead
alone, there is no such word.

The aliveness I felt on knowing it's still here
the word heartwarming would be underrated.
This bloomed from a barren field
something in us nourished this in whole
it's blossoming the care
around you, there is a flair
to carry the broken pieces in me

and never let it disappear.

" To have someone like you in my life is way beyond what I asked for, or better - I only asked for you"

Hold YOU near

I traced down my fingers through his hair.
It was already covering his eyes,
his head on my lap.
As my voice played on the music track
we hold our hands, walked down
the memory lane
to recollect the pearl of reminiscence
from the shore of the sea of history.
There was silence, agony
imprisoned alphabet groping for a place
it only found the void
and even words couldn't fill it in.

Afternoons had our conversation
on the branches, meeting the sunrays
and the mist all along.
Growing the leaf of smile
like a new beginning, it's spring already.
With your crinkles, ours blossomed like daffodils.
It brought back the mixtures
they love it when our names meet.
You are tiny, or the tiniest
I look down at you to see the grin
passing by your liplines.
Beautiful you are in these colours,

you will glow even when we grey out.

" People usually ask why I'm always smiling and enjoying this life, I tell them it's because of my you my sweet cheeks "

I behold his curls, it's not as curly as it was
but the gaze never changed
you still look at me like you are
protecting me from the evil eyes.
I shuffled your hair
you say I always act like your mom
and I love that to grace.

If I ever get to surrender
I'll only bend my knees before you love.
I've seen the bleeding words through your writes
I pressed the volume high
It left the neighbours shut their ears
but I see no lame in making this high.
Will this last, at times I asked
to hold you near till the last
no matter how long till we long
and it's not less than forever, I know.

We pressed our hands against on another
lips met like growing petals
eyes searched the depth of our vision
we looked as if there is nothing left.
Will it survive the flood of rain
I know how to paddle with you on boat

I won't let the flow cover you face
even in the toghest tornado, we will spare
full of this in tiny pieces
to complete the puzzle in full chance.

The bridg has stood upon
bricks on the line, made the perfect path
between the towns, I'd travel down
swim across the ocean. run through the road
fly by the sky to hold you near.
We saw the future just like we knitted
around the meadow, where
the green would meet the azure
The dove stretching the wing length
freedom to hold you near.
We surfcaed the staream unsunk
passed the flames, unburned
we've been told to part
but will never let go the hold,
it is meant to hold you near.

" There are absolutely nothing and nobody that makes me feel this way except you my baby cakes "

Let's Not BREAK APART

Promised call
where I looked into the screen
unmoved, a touch could feel your voice
on the other end, refused
only remained the ones and zeroes.
The dashes connecting the line, like it
would connect with the other end,
unreachable, I surmised.
The ring, awaited
it rang again, I answered
not knowing the weeping through the speaker
'You promised' lightning in my head
sore down the depth.
'I know, I was trying' - the slipped sentence
had the tear of a sad poetry
incomplete - you continued
picked the dictionary and searched for words
and meanings to strike off.

The digital machine, closer to my ears
distances reduced, miles to meters
every look I recalled, how you looked away
I remembered - silence constructing
the art of not willing, caring
yet again not showing.

Spaces apart we stood, infinity - I wrote
goodbyes were on the line, it greeted
on the door, while you were tying your shoes.
You didn't look up
sadness ran down your cheeks
I caught a replica of what I had in me too.
Structured cushions, awaiting
scented candles, pensive.
You chose the side, stood with it
I still looked into your eyes
even when you looked away.

The tickets, booked
places apart. still we emerged
closer than how it was, your legs met mine
I smiled knowing nothing changed between us.
We shared moments with our secrets
in front of the crowds, still, we laughed
your memory of us, it painted butterflies
in my heart - you stammered on that topic
ours's in particular
Moving like a child, you searched for me
even on the vast surface
stood closer, what If I'd get lost.

When it was nearly over,
we had a moment in the space
between the walls, ceiling within us
Your palm on my cheek, till you saw
my breaking vein
Promised, inconsolable on the edge
of no tomorrow, paper bags

the loudest cheers, cuddling in the cushions
it all flashed back - I wonder if I turned Monalisa
Not recreating the smileless-smile, but somehow
'There is a road ahead, your's to be fair
to tell the world who you are, you alone'
Sweetness in voice
bliss to my ears, I heard
only this to say, I replied
'Let's not break apart' - don't count
the lines to a dot now
It should extend to the clouds
to the riverside, let's not break apart.

YoU and Me

Was it destiny, you and me!
the stocking and the suspenders
the shade and feathers of what I call - love
the together spend nights
to togetherness afterwards.
All the silly dances, and my head upon
your shoulders - your palm showering
shelter to my wanetred thoughts.
My knowledgebook, how you taught
half the passge unknown, still you read
in your terms, made it easier
for me to know.

The nakedness, I was never shy
wrapped within your arms, warm
enough to freeze the moment, abed
aside your tiny fingers, I was still a teenager
so were you, age never counted
two wasn't a mark, I swear.
To thank destiny for what was played
how it played, yet again on your side
this time you in my arms,
circling when the tape was recording
to keep it for the future,
I carried you out of the eyes,

never took away my touch from yur skin
I searched for your gaze
I found it almost everytime.

What to call it - my first love
it has your nameeverywhere out loud
slipped out of my tongue enought imes
brotherly affection, once there was.
I never said I hated that, to have
someone like you to share my demons,
my fear, to hold me tight when the fireworks
make room for the louder cries
your grip on my hands all through the night.
The paths changed, this turned mutual
I was waiting for the colour change
and you painted that in you too
my first wish to call you mine
and I did - it was always me and you
noone between.

Wiped away my tears, I doubted
all the roads, you became my map
the voice cracked - you held me tight
a nod to calm my stormy side
it was raging from the northern side
shed tears on the go
crimson red on the firmament.
'It's alright little champ'
you've been my favourite fan
Clicked the camers, quoted one day
I'll be known, thw orld will wear my name
an era will rise to witness that.

Every rain, you stored the waters
take pain, wear it, it will make you stronger
I recalled.

It was true indeed
you made me strong, I asked for nothing but us
you and me, in this place
to witness the stars, to count int down
to portray the true love onto the sky
to paint our story in those walls
high ahead, so they will know
it was between us and will always
remain amongst us
It's you and me

What You LOVED

Where we came from, how it began
circle arts, in and out
byhearted lines, voice high, termed out,
paced forth, the crown didn't wear our name
Holding hands on the screen
the screams deafened the ears
for the better, clapping high
they shed the tears, the day we passed
we worthed it, didn't we!

Agreed forth, years crossed
records broken, still we fly, far above
the mountain tops, you got it back
in another name, what you always loved.
In another chair, to witness the talent
once we were there, to read the lines
to read between the chamber of hearts
A place of all the beginning, where we parted
your hands, my grip, how we suffered
how we emerged, a platform of our future number
Just a few kids from the village side
The story gave us life, pages on our names
headlines, now it's your turn
Proud is a small word, find me a synonym
for this better stage of life.

Soundcheck, hair cut short
the soldier look, sharper I said
checked shirt, your favorite near the chair
the feedback on the go, how they cheered
your name in loud, to notice the stand out of all
not to separate the colored hands in hold
you did sink into the depth of certain tunes
your eyes wet, I remember it used to fill
from the time I knew - words cracked
you disappeared into lost thoughts
managed the circle like your own
the cool guy tag, you love it
lead the voice to the throne,
who once was victorious
You smiled for those in need
connected the chords to complete.

It brought back the memories
the white building, the teddy bear
I cuddled hidden in the glass door
still I visited, away from the flashes
You grew your hair, a bit longer
learned to cut the tomato, a surprise to my spirit
For the curtained stages, you've seen us
ours sang the lines, unstructured
the golden buzzer, and your white shirt
how you still remain my golden guy,
the tressure wherever I begin,
I end with you for the better.

What you loved between the walls
of life and the road

another remark to shut the news
the talk behind the back.
Yours is my favorite voice
the soothing rhythm of my hour
the beating waves of my seconds
It's back for you from the closed doors
the intentionally shut ones
We belong to a place we loved
what you loved is what I loved
for another year, for another journey
the title got your name on it,
it is another color, isn't it!
When I'm not home, you are not home too
Oh, I'm here to see you on the chair,
smiling at me when I'm solo
standing for your mind to see the halo
we made on top of what we loved
It's safe here in this place
visible to the lovely deeds of the day.

Lost In YOU

Life painted the crimson red
in its horizon aloft
I recall seeing your face
turned red like that back then.
The fallen petals of the summer shine
found new beginning from the drizzle of love
Downpour met the valley,
your stem bowed, you didn't see
the spring for anyone else
The count spin in its axis
one more time, the calender pages
furled the days like in a hurricane.

Why didn't you talk
the words never reached the shore.
I will wait even in the flooding rain
for you to sail me home,
to see that smile waking me up
like the morning sun rays.
You taught me to count the stars
in the most lumiest night,
I still remember you saying
" No matter how far they are,
they will shimmer their eyes at us "

On the grass field, with our back aganist the grasses
on the top of buildings

Stepping Out

The voice echoed
the message beeped
a moment between us, flashbacks returning
words aimed, got hit, three injured
unintentional - it was from my end.
The cracked openings on the other side
left you wounded, every arrow
arrived on two ends hurt the two in line
where I remained silent, the reason for it all
blame me for that.
The phone hit the floor
the call line was still on, everything slowed
I saw the earth reversing
memories fading, broken screen
'You should've told me' - broke off from your chest
the voice trailed off,
I shouldn't have put my skin upon him, I know
mute I went, no words dropped.

Bags packed, you stormed out of the house
eyes teary, not looking onto my side
It did hit you hard, to know
that my heart did once bent for another soul
who once was your friend too.
I tried to make you stay, you stepped out

telling me 'You will regret this one day'
regret was already clouded in my life
the moment I decided to keep the secret
away from your reach.
Never I thought the call' would arrive
that you'd pick up
that the voice on the other end would call my name
that you would recognize the caller
with no confusion on the state
everything was delivered, you stood hearing
the pieces being thrown at me
still silent waiting for your chance to reveal.

The headlight of the car dimmed,
you shut the door, ill
I placed my hand on the windowpane
begging you to stay
where everything I wished for
was now being taken away.
The vacuum inside, le no part
of my voice in, you kept your vision
to the steering, lost in thoughts.
Smacked, it didn't break
shield down, I was ready to surrender
no chance given...
The wheel drove off, from the top of my lungs
I called out you to stay
but I saw you stepping out
from the doors, shutting
from my hands, retreating
from my hug, grieving

eyes not in the way to catch mine
it already passed down the hill.

If You DON'T LOVE Me

Spattered tears on the floor
I stood in front of your door, knocking
eyes clouded by the seasonal change
of an hour back, I drove in search of you
in the parking lot, I saw the same number plate
the door opened in distaste
yours were reddish, eyes and cheeks
the background story of
you were crying in the drive,
inside the room, the space between us, counting
the distance, vast and deserted.

Stretched my arms to surround your
tiny shoulders, you shrugged off
two steps back, I felt the depth
I sunk down, on my knees now, apology on my heels
'Please don't fight with me, I'm sorry'
pretension cut my throat, I deserved every bit
of it all, a spasm in my words
it throttled - call me a cheater
at least for once, I was one,
spate on the floor, uninvited
you broke off to the cushion with
palms covering your face.

If you don't love me, there is no
paths ahead, I'd call it a day
and never come to light, I'd let my
words hang on the ceiling for you to tear apart
I'll show you my heart then you decide.
It never fell for one, I swear
It had always been you,
please don't color me blank
If you don't love me, there is no way around
I hear your cries.

" I'm drowning in the ocean of silence between us "

It falls on me, the voice on the other end
of the line, he called your name
told me you've been always his
and the lines verified - words entangled
smothered me half, I can't hate you
but tell me how to love again.
Sunset in my life, it was dark already
now it's darker, no sight of light
I've been cheated, not to use that word
but 'It is what it is' I've seen it
Back then, you had his hands
wrapped around your shoulders
he placed that in me too
how to vanish this speck,
it's written all over your face.

Leave me to the ground, I'll dig me
a place down, put mud on my face love

I'll leave it like that, so you won't recognize
me anymore - I'll keep the mouth shut
you won't hear me screaming with pain,
the broken heart can't be healed that way.
I choose nothing over you
you choose someone over me
I'll pick the bricks and trap me in
The innocence in your eyes spilled
the love for someone else
I'm revolving in this spindle, I can't
read a verse - never knew the love
you placed on someone's heart would
sprout, it's growing strong
I've heard it in his splutter.

Not thinking the bending knee would help
it's spinning in my head
the reverse of all we had, it was never me
I'd walk with you till the end
but this is the end, out you go, will you!
Shut my eyes, lights out
blinding pain, sore throat, and a squabbled heart
searching for the conversation.
Don't think it is worth it
tears ran down my cheeks,
you were fully on the floor, crying
I didn't hear, intensional
I can't hear a thing song sang
Both our thoughts shrieked,
veins dead, turned red, stabbed from the back
I won't survive...
Two broken pieces on two sides

it won't get repaired, now I know

" I had someone once who made every second mean something. And now.... I am lost, unsure what to call this "

I'M SORRY

No one was prepared for the war
it broke out from naught, there is no stop now
petals down, when will it blossom again
like it used to, let the dews on top of it
to paint its nails, the stars ahead
to shimmer for the promises we made
It's written, not faded. the kite of love
out from the thread, wandering directionless
Beaks on the skin, vultures ate the quarter
rest flows in the air, bleeding
how will it sing like it used to
apples, eaten dead, red to the veins
will it break, poisonous words could get
injected onto the chambers
survival, will it find its way

Eyes found no sunny day
it's been raining all week
I remember how you used to wipe it
aways every time I had this
Loneliness crept in, into the woods
like a stray dog I ran
behind me, spades and swords
to rip apart - another apology rejected
treated ill, it's not like it used to

back then you used to look at me
without catching my eyes
now there is no you aside
I perforated your heart, there is no
love like this, peerless it sounds
I'm sorry, will I be forgiven I doubt

Coated in insecurities I once floated
randomized the struggle, whatever I picked
it pointed to the wrongdoing.
It was just another play around the corner
don't take it for granted
that shade of blue I painted
the land in green and yours on the hill
Horns louder, wiper binding
still the mist of fog on the glass
I couldn't see you standing still
a million times I can fall on my place
and tell you to forgive, will there
be mercy on your end.
Is it forceful on your end to shut me out
the painting on the wall, talking
about the stories we once shared
It shifted, from one to two
the two of us, should we make it
till the end.

FOREVER Is Not Real

Typewriter stopped,
ink flows through the paper
mixed with the older songs and
tinted the lines with gold.
Our giggles tingled in repetition,
a whit of how we were
Beyond the satisfactory tation
forever was booked, we traveled
bid for the favorite spot
here we were, in the arms of one anotn=her
till dawn, unseparated.

How to quote today
how to make me hear music
when I'm already deaf, how to deal with
the deflation of myself - it told me
forever was not real.
Let me out in the air like a balloon
hydrogenated, it flew higher, pointless
the arrows deflected, pointed to an unknown
destination, it stopped, cracked open
got hit with a rock, above the clouds
particles of a life i dreamt
fall onto the depth of the ocean, vast
how to stay closer to forever

when it is not real.

I put the passage back into the box
unread, searching for you to remove
the envelope - pasted with the love of
how you tasted, wrapped by the color of
how it lasted, play the music in your head
and dance along with me in your arms
like the one we played with a beer in your left hand
with me on your right one dancing in circles
Have you forgotten the steps
in contradiction to what we knew
understanding communication is not found

Rainbows disappeared, no light
I paddled between the stars to reach the moon
I was wrong after all
It is afar like the 'forever'
I'll sink myself into the black hole
so I'd never prove forever is real, wrong
It blinked, I saw your eyelashes
how you used to wake me up
shine through your side whispers in the air
no one to tell me we were rare
we were true, unique.
Here I am, sitting with crossed legs
typing with shivering fingers
it searched for your name only.,
I'm used to that side of the machine
I wonder if that had a memory
I wish this forever would stay
if this could be real again.

Coldness In LOVE

Frozen, I sat on the floor barefoot
back against the door closed
angels bought me a piece to wear
looks so white on the go
Windows clapped, piano running
on its own, the chandelier lighting up
lighting out, no stability, just dimmed
Cells remained ill
heart stood without a chance
everything changed.
Now there is a coldness in this love.

Knocked, someone had to open the door
wasn't locked, they mocked
I threw myself to the floor
crashed against the tiles
red letting out from my eyes
it rained, all the memories heavy
for my arms to hold
I let go, there is a coldness in this love
painted with the pain of another heart

Smacked fist, against the mirror
I sensed it in my knuckles
the grain of broken pieces, digging deep

to the path to let us fall
to let us out from the hold
I don't know, separation on the foot
walking in, I won't let go now
will you stay...
Warm me up against
the coldness in love

" I will always be next to you, close to your heart, please let me in "

Searched for you in places
can't utter the words
I disappeared onto the zone, alone
to make a boat out of my soul
to sail away, from this emptiness
to forget how you lied with
all the smile on your face
I'm frozen, there is a coldness in this love

I didn't make the call
trembling, the typing went wrong
didn't press 'send'
I was ill before the sunset
I didn't wait for the sun to rise
wrapping me in a woolen tide
freezing outside, intended convos
the staged art to fool me
there is coldness in this love
Will I ever survive?
" Thinking of you, always my sweet heart "

All You Did Was SAVE ME

The lines in the air remained
left my hand hanging in the air
filled my eyes every minute of the hour, still, I wrote.
Unfinished, our story exclaimed
places my heart on the paper
so you could hear what I was waiting for
When the piano finished off another
I found our love tangled up
within the seats

I was still in my bed to have seen
the darkness of this loneliness
I blame myself for that, for the time
I left without a goodbye
the stream of water down my body
the ache of shadows creeping in shaking
tripped inside another yell of myself
I should've known better.

So long ago, you had me in your arms
when the tears rolled down
you pulled me to your chest
I was told to let go of my fear
aside you, I found my safest place to hide
'You are strong' you told me all the way

Hid nothing, I was open to your kisses
you held my hand, protecting me from
all the flashing lenses,
never blinded my vision
I was asked, questions out of my sight
I answered, your name was in it

I see you walking by
there are no calls till now,
yet I knew I should make, I never did
All went blank, flags on the broken branches
not knowing how to wave
stretched my hand to get a hold
found another centimeter ahead
Fear, it drew my picture
with a black pencil, shaded me out
there is no color in me now.

On the shelf, I've seen the picture
we took twelve calendar turns aback
your smile, I'm waiting for it to find mine
I'll know someday
I looked out the window, did your
the car passed by, with khaki shorts and
shirt white ran down the roads
I was falling outside
it was already falling inside
I kept my voice inside a barrel
shut, open for me when in time.

When you closed the door
for your heart to grow

all you did was save me
you shut me out to make me strong
yu faded out, to let me in
you stepped back, so I could step in
you closed the curtain for me to open
you greyed out the colors, told me to paint
Here I stand, like a rainbow half
still on the ridge to fall
all you did was save me

The thread is all broken, here I go now
wandering, around the clouds, the kite
it will be torn apart in this hurricane
They traced their hands around my chest
how to identify, I'm lost in your sight
you are the only vision visible to me now

I'll know someday
how to apologize, to hold your hand
and stay likewise to kneel down my knees
for the forgiveness, I'm searching
The dip of every road, the cracked openings
on the walls, I'll know someday
how to fix a broken heart.

Is It Too HIGH

The fringes, still cover my hazy eyes.
To begin from where we left
here I try, the parted ways to converge
walls too high, now coming down
I only have the door
will you build me a home!
The picture of your voice
it haunts me now, smile
I bid it to someone in need
will you help me find it back!

Every sunrise remained sunset
Woken up from sleepless-sleep alone
Holding onto the space beside
it's empty like a river left in drought.
All the coffee cups left a stain,
of the tasteless yesterday
The smoke of the thoughts in my head,
I'm breathing only the dead particles in place.
It grew till my shoulders, the hair
to see your reflection when I look in the mirror.
I can't find my clothes
for all I'm seeing is yours...
I shut the cupboard pretending
to have lost the key which is still in my hold

Walked away, forgot to revisit till now
all the pages we read, when did you mark them unread!
Climbed all your ways higher
I stood watching, blurred vision
the stairways took away, I'm still here
looking at you - forgiven for what it took
to place your heart on the line
and called it a fine one,
when it was not.

Lights out, searched for something I lost
in daylight, found half a heart
it had the rhythm of what's inside mine
All the celebrations for tomorrow
here is a gift, I kept aside my sorrow
pulled the sheets out, wrapped in my name
will you read it out loud
for you to hear
It's us, I hope a comeback.

In a place, memories shared
I quoted the name, if you'd recognize
will you write me a letter!
For every note left unsaid,
for every tear held back
for every ache in the heart
we deserve another chance.
Another count to add up to yours
Is it too high to come down,
if you remember this phase, hum the lines
if you still see our faces, run back to me
I'm still here, down to the ground

no fences, it's only me now
I'm still here to run my fingers through your curls
run back to me... hold my hand.

3 AM

Dropped another glass
on the ground, it sprinkled
All dried throat wanting no drop of hope
searched for a soul, deep within
I call a sound, I'm all muted
The days, passed
another fall on the riverside
ripples let the lines reach the shore
it was for you to make a boat
frozen now, wish I could be the snow
so I'd float all my ways to you
when it melts, over the top of our roof.

Through the streets, I walked
all the signs told me of you
How to unsee the pictures we drew
will fade away, it won't
can't win a conversation on this board
for I know, it's painted with our gaze
How to look away when the eyes already met
I parceled a present for you in words
I hope it reached your postal code.

You blew off the candles, you weren't here
all through the midnight, I waited

a shiver of relief, knowing you care
it's 3 AM, no calls awaiting
still near the curtains, I see the silhouette
of the hugs we had the last time around
I'll step onto the place, for your eyes to behold
Corners whispering the stories we told
We grew another year old
still young to each other's hold.

From where we belong, to how it goes now
the tread of pain, I've seen it in your eyes
In words of slowness, the rush of coming back
The bushes outgrew, the fences have taken their spot
off from the ground floor.
A knock on the door, I expect
a card full of wishes, you wrote...
Feels the same, for a decade
we remain the identical as what it was,
the azure sky above, it's half-past five
dropped to the floor, it was me again
and over again...

It's BETWEEN us

Started car, its only the sunrise
up in the hills of the written stars.
Horns collided, mine survived, focus on the glass,
dew being washed back by the wiper blades
Steering wheel turning, parking light evading,
there is still a claimed art on the street lamps.
Are they just like me.....
Searching for blue in the reddish arch?
Under the branches...
will the birds sit and sing all the songs as I sing now?

Here is to chase down,
all the miles apart, can't measure
how to quote all the conversations,
now being trapped in these lonely chases.
Dipped my head to the road, it's all in my zone,
path declining, hours fading, still I drive
to chase it down, to make it far
to the reach, where you belong.

Slowed down, stopped engine
like my heart, still pumping
Pushed the door open, got out
I'm out in the middle of an empty road.
The phone, beeping

pretended to have not heard it.
It kept on, with the ringing
I swear I didn't hear.
Out as like a wandering breeze
hoping to find the leaf
to blow his fringes and my curls
I'd chase down like I'm the chase

Knocked, no answer at the first
Knocked again, why can't you just open!
Fall, onto the doorstep hoping you'd open up...
Not of the times, we talked
Not of the plays we played
Not of the hugs and kisses
Not of the longest walks
It all came down to this, the silent call,
it all falls down to this it's not my call...
but yours in pieces.
Flew off the ocean, ran down the riverbeds,
lay down in valleys
capturing what remained.

It all comes down to this chase
Not of the calls we made
Parted hands in places,
yours on my shoulder now, misplaced
Mine on your rainy cheeks
Still holding, eyes to eyes
gaze to the depth, heart to heart
do I need to whisper
Now it all comes down to this.

Leaned closer to the walls,
misspelled conversations rearranged,
words replaced, no punctuations ending.
Voices grew from the valley to the hilltop,
from flat to the frequency lines, curving.
On top of the lungs, giggling.
Eyes on the shine, through the ceiling
Coffee is served in the mug
should we drink it cold, or do you still like it hot!

Still, on the counter of this room,
you sit like a child, making no conversation
still, we kept our eyes on the sunny side of the shore,
not knowing how to chain the letters into words,
tangle the coldness into this phase,
trace the fingers over the sink like we used to.
Coffee cups, staring at the steam escaping,
should we escape too, to somewhere afar...
I've been waiting for this moment
like the seasonal change,
leaves falling, flowers blooming,
under the surface of these floating changes,
we always look the same,
unmoved and unmistakable...

Called your name,
from a hand distance,
hands easing from the taste of the bittersweetness
Birds flew back, in search of shelter we call,
pendulum swinging, hands clutched,
a door half open and into the spinning disc,
lights out, it's between us, there is no space.

Tape recorder, music playing,
hands tied to the movement, dancing.
Let out a sigh, It's between us,
never felt safer than these arms surrounding mine...
It's between us.... honey
It's between us.

All the PLACES TOGETHER

Seat belt tight, to keep you steady
Windowpane, black from outside
no eyes intruding, still we see the haunting flashes,
cameras shutting, captured not we believe.
Hoody in place,
covered with no tattoos to be seen,
the couple ones, you got it only days
after I placed mine, I remember.
The crowd on the line, you sneaked in
Have they seen us, we wondered
still, we sang our favorite songs.

Beaches, footprints, tasty tacos
Night ride, night club, grasses, dewdrops
traveled down the countryside, City lights,
greenery, and the azure sky...
Your friend's wedding, long hair, and black suit,
tiny and you are still cute...
Hid from the ground floor, stayed up on the rooftop
till the moon came up, and we find our reflection in each other's mirror,
whitened by the care, like a dove
Wine glass, date night,
just like the first time - polished nails shine,
olive branches, stars glazing, we only saw us

all the places together, hide and seek in the background.

Rolled over to your side,
arms around me abed, sheets dropping
night eavesdropping, groping over the weakness,
curled up tendrils shaking, curtains closing,
leaving this moment to only us.
Let's follow the fireflies, mangroves, and coral reefs
Let's not pace forth,
know we are slowing down...
we never got the chance to slow down back then.

You stood behind the bushes,
bandana around my neck,
another ride on the road,
this time you'll be there on the top floor.
Bags packed, shoelaces and no socks,
labeled I've been, cleaned up a bit,
still there is your cloth on the floor spreading...
pushed back to the wardrobe,
you don't care how you look,
one can't be more beautiful than you...
Unanswered questions they found,
another headline is made up,
I kept you away from the shuttering lights
all the places together, not revealing,
safer under my arms,
I'm safer within yours.

Your EYES

Trees grew in height, the shade of trust
the elevator door opened, you walked in
shirts in hangers, chairs spinning
My hands in the glass pane, looked out.
The buildings stood higher, vehicles running
for life, beyond the speedometres.
Jacket covering your t-shirt, focused to infinity
you stood, hands across your chest, thinking
I sunk into the abyss, not knowing the way out
your picture, recognizable on any night

Ocean blue, the chasms of life seen
grief and love in lanterns, brightening.
You smiled with your eyes, even in the rainy dusks
You've seen the artistry of missing
without looking, took away the glimpses
for someone's orders, you were torn
never let it pass down to me.
Defensive of all the hearts kneeled closer to yours,
took the chance to paint you out in black
you painted me in with angling lights
told me to hold it high.
Watched and loved the thread
of treating the rest with care
still, you suffered all the way along.

The mansion, and the waterfalls
the roses and noises
into a suit, you've changed
I was still in my floral shirt,
flipping the pages, the album
bed all shuffled, skinny jeans.
In the mirror, they've seen you
looked aside, there is your smile
narrowed eyes, ocean blue
hair covering your temple, adjusted.

How the night, you were taken away
private planes and signed pieces
tearful eyes, when you return
distancing from me since then, I didn't know why
I gazed into your eyes
hid beneath the styled strand of hair
looked away, walked apart, stood outlying
Restricted, my hand retreated
you shuttered, never heard a sob
deep inside, you were crying I know

Raised eyebrows, I converged
Explanations, and my nose scrunched
held back a laugh, no eye contact.
Decorations, white roses
ribbons and cakes, all the pretty chairs
candles, and wines, corridors dividing
emerging into a hall
Picturesque the moment, you were coming down
all grinning, hearts met, you dug your head

into my chest, hugged and kept it the way
the silly knee touches, the delicate gazes
our little riddles, unknown to the masses
One day, something we always need.

I've seen the world through your eyes
felt the need to be seen by your eyes
I used to stare at your lashes
where I couldn't count the exact, still I try
Jumped off the ground, into my arms
I carried you out through the glints
Bumped into destiny, in a corner of the lavatory
I knew you were a beam of light
even back then...
lighting up the darkness
all in angles, inclined, put my arms
on your thigh, held my hand
walked me out of the airport all days
I've been walking down memory lane.

We Will Survive

All the ashen Sundays,
heart-ripping chant's stain
immaculate eyes hissing at the sinners
I can see myself in,
crosses on the neck,
I don't fear the knells,
a rope around my neck, trying, throttling
Choked onto what's this picture holds
saviors of the mankind, they asked for the man
out of my dress, kempt in manliness
They are illuming the world, I never knew
set ablaze to one's self, buried him alive
lighting the world by the fire of someone's heart

Got rebuked, kept the distances
like a country away
Not to look, warnings and shouting.
Papers signed, they plundered our innocence,
made the call, it's the image to be shown,
no loud cries, no protest,
Skinny jeans, and shirt open
Clouds arrived, they never disappeared,
haunted to every edge, sleepless nights,
fearful mornings, like in a mourning
we shed tears, hidden behind the curtains,

blinded by the lights, it merged with the sweat,
no one knew our eyes were full.

Parted ways, in every way we searched,
for this heart to go home, to learn love,
to love one's self, not to call it by a name
uniqueness is not to be blamed
I found my love in you, you found that in me too,
same but they opted for the written opposite,
revealed not to reveal
knew, but they don't know, how to say it's alright,
we are the sinners
in their eyes, call us the sinners
but we will survive
Left with me is a sad clown
still, I laugh at the prattling headlines that we don't like
they don't know what they're saying,
but they say it all the time.

I scud away, caught behind
I've been trapped, you survived
Left the lines, quoted in, painted blank,
held the flag, placed my heart in the middle,
drained my beats till it breaks, it didn't
We will survive like the stars
No darkness, only the light, and rainbow,
you the blue, I'm the green,
rest we know what to feel
We will survive...

Are We Enough

Closed curtains and carpool
rendezvous and long walks
Peeking through and eyes shut
darting away from the gazes
KItchen floor, and the water droplets
you dropped off the second last day
Jumped into the bed, fall off the roof
into the waterbed, we swam alongside too
damped hair and chuckled through.

My dimples and your crinkles
I looked down, you looked up to me
Fear, you washed it out for me
You stood in front, to keep the arrows away from me
no armor you wore, still, you took it all
No canvas and brushes
you painted all with your emotion.
Having seen the lights red, you never stopped
carried me out till I see the green
Of all the casual talks,
every single one is my dearest.
Of all the broken pieces,
I still can see the unbroken bond

Are we enough, we asked it all the count
out of all the precious times
Are we enough, we knew the answer right
it was never out of the line
Are we enough, to take the stars
and plant amongst the place of the heart
Are we enough. to keep this all alive
till we last, till the tides never run back.

" I gazed into him, I saw the world, picture-perfect "

Face to face, out of nowhere
hand in hand, like the long wait
running down the stairways
we feel the childishness emerging
I dressed you up, princess smile
heels, you tapped the floor in style
polished nails, another round
bow in your head, we've danced
rings and your pretty fingers
I miss your curls, but you are the same
on my shoulders, sleeping
No tears to be shed, I'm here

Drove too fast, you're not scared
here in this bar, drinks shared
another round you just glared
at the seat behind us,
not letting you stretch your legs
Your arms around my shoulders
mine wrapped around your waistline

we walked until the sun meets the curves
of the mountain above the ground.
We are enough for the ways
we are enough for the days
even if we are not, we are enough
for you and me, isn't it enough *happy*

" Honey, I know life is a challenge, there are so many hindrances on the way, ones that are unpredictable. I promise to love you forever no matter the circumstances "

To LOVE and to NEVER Let Go

No more traffic lights to stop,
keeping the steer in hand, steady
No fast-forwarding from reality
let's slow down and catch the sky
changing colors every time.
Climb the tops, feel the cinch
Big Ben ticking the numbers,
passenger trains, and private jets
can we go back to normal

Back in the grassy land
roll around the field, go higher the Eifel tower
and see the life in real
Run down the roads together
you will win I know, you've been
the champion in this little run, I proudly hear.
Broke an arm, hospital room crummy - you complained
Still, you jumped off the higher grounds
kept the hand away from the sling
chased down the time
and the planes, you made it

Against the flashlights, I looked for your face
haven't seen the silhouette
searched every corner for my little freak

Caught your eyes, stuck my tongue out
danced alive, harder than they see
Lines, broken has been tied
Grudge, all those left was evanesced
Thrown words, taken back
we said it couldn't, but we took it back
No more tears in this ride

Simplified,
I swapped your last name with mine
Alongside the thread, it sounds
The prince's name in the middle
are we about to build our kingdom,
glass windows, arch doors,
and the perfect view
up in the balcony of our palace
Anchor and rope,
without you, there is no me.
Compass and the ship,
how will I sail without your direction?
We wore the masks,
hid behind the unknown, here we are
imprinting your name on me.

Waves, fireworks I used to fear
Closed eyes and treasure,
glowing face of yours...
Dressed up in suits, tensed we were,
no piece of paper needed
Rings exchanged, I was already yours,
you were already mine
Twenty did count, eight more added,

stars appeared, the sky was still light...
More clues and clueless nights,
stood away, two beds, no cuddles,
back to one bed,
small spoon and eyelashes counting.

Your temple and the shared kisses
Packed bags and unpacked ones
Wine glass and glass crumples
Lights out room, up in the building
I've seen you smiling
I watched you from higher
The bus, the sticker, how you cuddled
into my chest, a safer place.

Here we stand, to love and never let go
to rise from the bottom and never stop
Cleared sky, the rainbow arrivals
how we fastened the seatbelts
and looked up, it's all certain now
All the cries, all the places,
up all night, till the AM four in the morning
talking about the memories we made
at the midnight...
Will it take us home?
it will take us home to love and never let go.

Your name on me,
like the drizzle in the desert,
like the green leaf in the autumn,
like the ripples carrying the paper boat,
like the dews, the sprout, and seeds.

Your name on me
like the shining of the stars,
the Pearl-like moon, the free birds,
the open cage, freedom to wear your name
Another sunrise, ours to ours
Your name on me,
my name on yours,
to last till the last

The World Will Know

Are you prepared to tell the story?
Twelve counted, should we wait for more?
Started off, keeping on
driving the highways,
turn right to the countryside,
hands inside the sleeves,
looking out to the line
where the green meets the blue
where I meet you...
no more hiding.

I need you inside my arms
when I walk through the crowds,
I need you up here facing the waving lights,
you take the flag, will you!!
Wave it out with pride,
show them your biggest smile,
wrap your arms around my neck,
let me pick you up like the first time,
let's spin around like in a dance ball,
why can't we be the last ones to leave this room
I'll carry you, like the feathers
I'll keep you like my breath
I'll write the story in our names.

The rhymes were written,
chords tuned in, halfway letter delivered
did it reach your side, the door was closed then,
opened halfway I was ready to let you in.
Tires arrived, passed the roads
you came in, it's ours now
All the love songs, the cloudy eyes,
your hands are taken into my heart,
no more fear to sing the life in the lines,
not sure how deep we will fall,
it's on the rope, still, we got the hold,
slipped to sides, broken chord,
still, we passed another stage in life.

The world will know,
A boy met a boy, fell in love with stars,
and my stars were you...
I counted off the stars,
so I could see the last one was you.
Kept all my skin away from them
so I could only be closer to you
The washroom stories of how we met,
the bedtime talks of how we loved the time around us,
you admired my curls,
kept me safe so I would never get lost,
all my trembling fingers and my dried throat,
all the painful nights and my torn soul,
you picked me up from the floor,
searched for me in all the sidewalls,
rescued me from the cage,
sacrificed yours...

" He is caring, he treats me really well, indeed "

I'm here, on the shore with you
We can sail off home and tell the world,
it's always been you
Can't wait anymore,
is it already late I wondered.
You lay on my lap, eyes closed
were you sleeping, I talked
Nodded your head,
a smile emerged from the corner of your lips
It's time we should let the world know.
Brushed your hair,
you put your foot into the water,
halfway freezing.
Warmed you with the silky cuddle in the tiny form.

I'll marry you now,
under the branches of this blue shaded sky
Wind be the chorus of this love song, being hummed.
I'll find you
even if you're trapped in a maze,
I'll carry you
even if I'm weak by the heaviness of the hate,
I'll guide you
even if I'm lost in the middle of a desert,
I'll follow you
even if I'm not strong enough to take another step,
I'll love you
even if I'm not going to love myself anymore.

Crumbled envelope of a love letter,

I've sent it my way and they rejected,
Told me to stay away from you, I guaranteed.
I slept in a bed of rock and swords
so they could give you the roses,
I hummed in silence so you could sing it loud,
I walked down the path so you could take the higher,
I played the bad so you could be the greatest.
Here we are, standing hand in hand,
to say to the world that we've been loved,
by the love of one another,
we've been haunted by the hate
they aimed at us when we were younger.

The world will know,
the blizzard we've come across,
was the strongest but we survived,
so love is the strongest of all
Flashing lights, headlines we don't care anymore...
We've been thrown out to the depth,
kept it likewise for years
still, we sang the song of this beautiful war,
we survived.
The world will know,
they should know, why wait, let it out
so we could recolor
the phases of this lifetime,
we could tell the world that
we were fighting out and we won

" My curly boy, my rainbow ... my sunshine "

HOME

Let me take you awaywhere the moon gleams beyond the skywhere the twilight would feel like a daylightwhere your resilience never failsThere is more to this worda story that unfolds, a connectionwithout another name, it's this word, I'll show you the road home

The silence ends,petrichor of another beginningpours like the rain in summerA drop to these dried throatsThe void disappearedfilled with the love of our longingno more prick in the airthis is where we belong, home.
It is where our hearts arewhere it said ' It will be alright'when the fences build 'I can't take it anymore' around us, this gave us the shelter of 'You are strong'Gone we were for so longforgotten we were, of the places we traveledof the promises and all the calls

Home has never been the samewithout you, it was a lonely cemeterywhere I'd wait for the gladioli to rebloom so I could pick the sword andmeasure the length of my heart tooWhen the descending dusk painteda cast of the shadow upon meI had perched over the footprints like a raven

Home has never been the samewithout you, I felt myself a lighthousesurrounded by the howl of the sea crashing against the sands of a heartwhich was already misplacedlittle gray light, bubbles of life floating atopI wondered why it never brokenever knew you were searching for this home

" We fought, let the silence answer the remaining questions, and the silence won over us in this run. As I stand here, looking into your eyes there is nothing I need more than keep you in my arms, to have your care protect both of us from whatever struggle we are gonna face. We will be fine ..."

In your graceful embrace, it was heldamiable to those written wordsanother door opened, reentrance to this lockedwhen did I find the key, which was lost!Let me take you awaywhere the birds would sing our songwhere the brook would reflect the moonwhere the hills touch the clouds

The hurt endsthere is no sheer sadness in our wayThe hunting eyes, they departedwe found the way back home, where we belongwhere we collided into each other's holdwhere everything seems to come to life at oncememories of us in repeatI turned back to you, I found home.

It is where our hearts arewhere we can love alone with usOnce it cut me down and stitched me upThe fallen years won't reappearstill, we thrive amongst each other's armsGone we were for many counts downforgotten we were, of all the starving winterof arm-in-arm and late-night tales

Home has never been the samewithout you, I felt the beat hindering downpaths diverging into the wrong sidecrests dropping to the ocean chasmI longed for the mantle of the tombstonewhere I'd freeze and worship the creepersmany feathers around my smile, singing the loneliest lullaby

Home has never been the samewithout you, I felt myself a swingwaiting for you to accompany, to set myself freeI was left hanging on my rusty thoughtsFor once you thought I'd let you fallI was selfless all along, I wish you knewall the brightest sunrise on the hills, I waitedand you knew, when I looked at you I found home.

" We found home in each other, when I left wounded I found him healing meself. Always in my heart, he will remain, we are enough and will always be "

Appendix

" One can't pretend to have lived a life that one hasn't lived, everyone waits for the society's acceptance to live this life the way they want it to be. In the end, all we carry would be a bag full of regret for not letting the world know who we were, what we were and who we loved, and how we loved. You can't and you should not pretend to be someone that you are not. Some people deal with an inconvenient truth about who they are by forming a second self to protect their real self, and then distinguishing between the two becomes difficult. You don't need to hide your sexuality, this place won't be lonely, if you still think expressing yourself is wrong, then it's time you should change your views. We cannot pull everyone to like us, or to accept us, but still, there will be at least one person, or some support to keep you going. Set yourself free, free from the cage, break off the glass closet, and keep your heads high."

YOU ARE BEAUTIFUL, KIND, and COLORFUL LIKE THE RAINBOW, always remember LOVE IS NEVER WRONG.

www.ingramcontent.com/pod-product-compliance
Lightning Source LLC
LaVergne TN
LVHW050418160726
843469LV00041B/1123

9789356106833